WHAT DEGREE DO I NEED TO PURSUE A CAREER IN HEALTH CARE?

RITA LORRAINE HUBBARD

ROSEN
PUBLISHING®

To my mom, Willena Nunn, LPN, who was the first in our family to earn a medical degree, and my sister, Judith Brown, RN, who followed in her footsteps

Published in 2015 by The Rosen Publishing Group, Inc.
29 East 21st Street, New York, NY 10010

Library of Congress Cataloging-in-Publication Data

Hubbard, Rita L., author.
What degree do I need to pursue a career in health care?/Rita Lorraine Hubbard.—First edition.
     pages cm.—(The right degree for me)
Audience: Grades 7–12.
Includes bibliographical references and index.
ISBN 978-1-4777-7869-2 (library bound)
1. Medicine—Vocational guidance–Juvenile literature. 2. Allied health personnel—Vocational guidance—Juvenile literature. 3. Allied health personnel–Study and teaching—Juvenile literature. I. Title.
R690.H83 2015
610.69—dc23
                                                                2014006850

Manufactured in the Malaysia

CONTENTS

INTRODUCTION

Whether your school years are behind you or you have a few more to go before you're free to explore life's possibilities, you've probably already begun to think about the career you will pursue when you're finally out in the world of work. There are many things to think about, like what type of job you need to live a good life, how much training you'll need to do the job well, who will hire you, how much you'll earn, and whether the job you pursue will remain stable even in a struggling economy. These are all important questions that may take some time to answer, but while you're pondering, add this consideration into the mix: if you feel you would thrive in a job that allows you to meet lots of people, touch their lives, and make a difference—all without necessarily needing a license or degree to begin working—the field of health care might be right for you.

By definition, the health care field includes providing any personal or medical service or supply that prevents illness or treats or manages the physical, mental, behavioral, and emotional health of one or more persons. The health care field is as broad as a mountain range, with well over two hundred career paths you can pursue. If

This young medical assistant meets new people and makes a difference in their lives through her job. Here, she monitors and documents a patient's blood pressure.

your first concern is salary, you should know that entry-level workers can still make a decent hourly wage. If you're more interested in a professional career, your salary can soar to heights you've never imagined before.

But before you explore the financial rewards, you must first determine whether health care is the right path for you. Liking people and wanting to touch their lives in some way should not be the only factor you consider when choosing a career path. There are many reasons that health care may be the field for you. You need only examine these reasons alongside your personal goals to see if any of them are a good fit. For example, as a health care worker, you'll always be in demand, so if you yearn for job security, this factor is a plus toward your decision. You can live anywhere you want after you earn your certificate or degree because every area in the nation needs good, skilled health care workers. You will definitely make a difference in people's lives, but if you don't particularly care for working with people, the health care field is flexible enough that there are plenty of other jobs you can do.

Another great thing about this field is that, according to the U.S. Bureau of Labor Statistics (BLS), "eight of the top twenty fastest-growing professions are in the Health Care industry." This means that our society continues to need more health care workers, plain and simple. So whether you choose to be a physician or a paramedic, a dietician or a certified nursing assistant, you will be welcomed into the health care field with open arms. All you need to do is decide which career path you want to pursue and how you want to get there—with a certificate or with a degree.

CHAPTER ONE

Certificate or Degree?

N ow that you know some of the great reasons for choosing a career in health care, your next step is to explore specific job descriptions to decide which jobs interest you and whether they require a certificate or a degree.

No matter what health care job you have in mind, a degree—or, at minimum, a certificate—will probably be necessary. Both of these prove to prospective employers that you have at least the basic skills to perform in the field of your choice. When prospective employers see your certificate or degree, they will feel confident about bringing you on as a member of the workforce. They will see you as someone who is serious about getting a job, keeping it, and doing it well. They will know that you are ready to address the medical, emotional or physical well-being of those who need your services, whatever those services may be.

Even if you choose a job related to medical records, for example, where you do not directly interact with patients, you'll still need a certain level of skills to do your job effectively. You would, for example, need good

College graduates with bachelor's degrees in fields such as nutrition science can complete a supervised internship, obtain a license, and go on to work in a hospital, nursing home, or residential facility.

writing, listening, and communication skills. You would need to know administrative and clerical procedures, and you would definitely need to know and understand medical terminology.

So, back to the original question: which is right for you, a certificate program or a degree program? Your answer will determine how long you will need to study before you can work in your chosen field and how much money you'll need to spend in order to finance your studies. But before we discuss these factors, it's best to differentiate between certificates and degrees so that you understand what each entails.

Health Care Certificate Program

A health care certificate program offers a streamlined course of study in which you (the student) will gain all the skills necessary to perform a specific job well. You can take your courses in person (e.g., in a classroom or building) or online, and once you are finished, you will be ready for immediate employment.

Because the field of study is more focused in a certificate program, you will typically be able to bypass both general education courses (e.g., literature and natural science) and core academics (e.g., English, mathematics, and social studies). Certificate programs typically do not take as long as degree programs, so you can move into the workplace much sooner than if you were pursuing a degree. However, the skills you gain can still be used as a jumping-off point for obtaining a higher certificate or degree further down the road because many of the course credits can be applied to other programs.

Certificates come in all levels. Some certificates prepare you to work at jobs that are lower on the employment rung, like a certified nursing assistant (CNA), who helps invalids or the elderly with their toileting needs. But some certificates are actually add-ons to an earlier education, like when a medical assistant gets a certificate that allows her to become a licensed practical nurse (LPN) or a registered nurse (RN).

Certified nursing assistants (CNAs) help their patients in many ways. This CNA is providing both entertainment and assistance by helping this elderly man cut out pictures for an activity at the facility where he stays.

These add-ons open doors to more and better opportunities. For example, you would probably have a better opportunity for advancement if you earned a certificate in cardiopulmonary resuscitation (CPR) or became a certified medical assistant (CMA) because you would "specialize" in certain skills or procedures. Again, a certificate is usually earned much faster than a degree. Some certificates can be earned in less

BASIC SKILLS NEEDED FOR A CAREER IN HEALTH CARE

Before you enroll in certificate classes, on-the-job training, or degree courses of any kind, you still need a set of core basic skills in order to enter the health care field. You will need to be in good health and have great physical stamina because the population you serve may be sick, feeble, or elderly. You will also need great writing and communication skills to document vital statistics, maintain health records, and pass messages from clients to physicians. Because many people's physical, medical, and emotional well-being may depend upon how they interact with you, you must exhibit a sense of professionalism and a good work ethic. Also, since you will most likely be working with people from all walks of life, you'll need great customer service skills and a heart full of compassion for those who need your help.

than a year, and although other certificates take longer, they are still usually earned much faster than, say, a two-year associate's degree.

Health Care Degree Program

A degree is for people who want "a more rounded education" that will train them in a wider range of

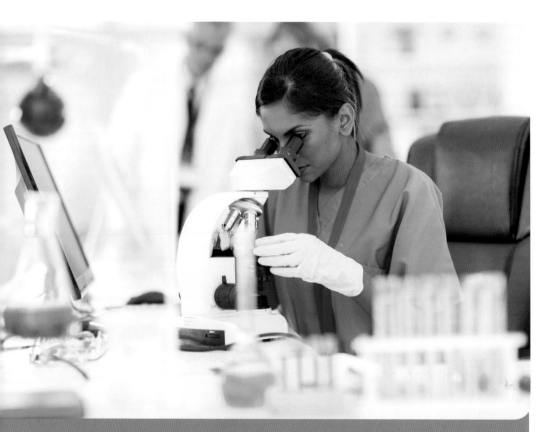

Pursuing a four-year bachelor's degree in fields related to medical science or research takes focus and determination. Courses teach students how to use a microscope and other laboratory equipment.

skills, take them further in their careers, and allow them to earn more money. This rounded education may include subjects like math, literature, English, or history classes—most of which are not typically required in a certificate program. A degree program, by definition, requires a much longer student commitment—sometimes multiple years. This required commitment has been known to discourage people who are eager to enter the workplace and begin earning money right away, but it usually pays off in the end because those who earn degrees generally earn much more over the course of their careers than those who earn certificates.

A degree can take anywhere from two years to ten years to complete. For example, a medical associate degree takes two years and typically prepares you for work in administration, medical records, or some type of medical office. A medical bachelor's degree takes four years and often involves learning to expertly use laboratory equipment. It can also be used as a bridge or stepping-stone toward an even higher medical degree involving clinical practice. A master's degree takes six to seven years (the four years required for the bachelor's degree and an additional two to three years for the master's program) and prepares you for a career as a researcher or educator. A professional doctorate takes even longer and prepares you for a lifelong career as a physician in the field of your choice (e.g., pediatrician or family practice).

In short, you can earn a health care degree in everything from nursing, family medicine, pharmacology, and

This committed young man invested many years to earn a medical doctorate degree and become a pediatrician. Here, he helps his young patient feel at ease while he takes his blood pressure.

podiatry to massage therapy, nutrition, internal medicine, and holistic medicine. Like certificate programs, some degree programs can be completed either in person (e.g., in a building or classroom) or online and can be tailored to fit your daily life schedule. However, because of the expertise involved, some degree courses must be completed in a lab, on location at a hospital or clinic, or in a classroom with face-to-face interaction.

CHAPTER TWO

Schools

Once you decide which program (certificate or degree) is right for you, you'll want to start thinking about where you will pursue your studies. There are some 1,600 colleges in the United States, so you have a lot to choose from. But how do you choose a school? How do you decide that one is better than the other? In most cases, you won't be able to differentiate; you'll only be able to determine what's best for you, based on your personal circumstances. You might ask yourself questions like how quickly you want to earn your certificate or degree, how far you're willing to commute to attend, whether there are grants or scholarships to help you fund your schooling, and what type of real connections the school has with the working world. You'll also need to ask yourself an even more important question: should you attend a two-year, four-year, or multi-year school?

Some students interested in a health care career will pursue four-year programs, while others will opt for two-year certificates and faster entry into the job world.

Two-Year Schools

Two-year schools have many names. They are called vocational colleges, technical colleges, and even junior colleges. They offer associate's degrees, continuing education courses, and adult education courses for those who just want to go back to school but are not seeking a degree or certificate of any kind. They also offer remedial education courses for high school graduates who are not quite ready for traditional college. In terms of certificate programs, they offer specialized training in fields like technology, nutrition, and occupational therapy assistance that may be completed in anywhere from six weeks to a year or more.

Vocational schools usually have open admission, which means everyone is welcome to enroll. These schools may be located in malls or stand-alone buildings and may have several branches in various areas of town so that they are convenient for everyone. They are typically less expensive than four-year schools and are quite flexible as far as scheduling. They offer day, evening, weekend, and online classes for the busy student. These courses often "cut to the chase," meaning they typically bypass the prerequisite and elective courses required by the four-year colleges and dive right into your specific field of choice. This fact in itself means that you would complete your certificate program or associate's degree much sooner than if you attended a four-year college.

Your certificate or associate's degree (depending upon the path you choose) would be your ticket to finding a job immediately after graduation, or at least faster than if you attended a four-year college. But perhaps the best part about attending a vocational school is that the credits you earn for the courses you take are usually transferable to a four-year college program if you decide to further your education at a later date.

Depending upon your goals, your cash on hand, and your particular circumstances, a two-year school may be for you.

Four-Year Schools

A four-year school offers both undergraduate and advanced degrees in a variety of fields. The curriculum includes more than just the core classes that prepare you to work in your field; it also contains broader courses, like math, history, literature, theatre, and so forth. A public four-year school (or college) is typically more expensive than a two-year vocational school, but it is still usually cheaper than a private college.

If you choose to attend a public college, you will need to complete a four-year course of study before you can obtain a degree and pursue a job in your field. Of course, there are always exceptions. For example, if you want to become an RN, you could take your courses while you work part-time as a nursing assistant or home-health aide in order to understand a typical workday in the medical environment.

You could apply for a range of in-state and federal financial aid to assist you in paying for your courses, and the degree you earn would reflect a more comprehensive course of study than the vocational degree. For example, you could become an RN or pursue a

Occupational therapy students can complete a certificate program at a two-year vocational college. This occupational therapist helps a patient recovering from surgery learn how to throw a ball again.

program that would lead to a bachelor of science in nursing (BSN). You could also become a scientist or even a medical researcher.

The differences between the two-year school and the four-year school are the length of time you need to take your courses, the amount of money you'll be required to spend, and the level of expertise you can expect to gain by the end of the courses.

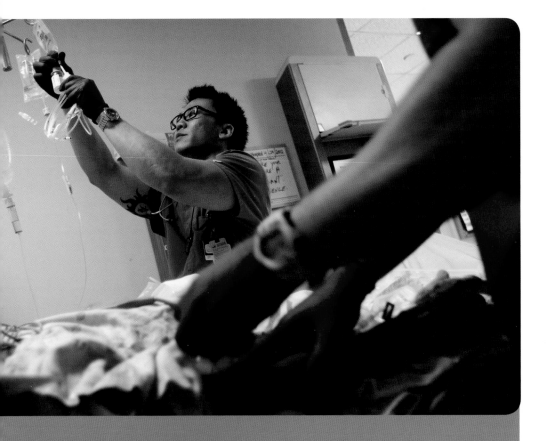

This RN gets plenty of practice being a bedside nurse. Here, he hangs an IV bag for one of his patients.

Five-Year and Ten-Year Programs

For the very serious health care student, the five-year-plus school or program may be a serious option. Here, you can go all the way. You can choose from a range of specialties, including medical doctor, scientific researcher, university teacher, or psychologist.

WAYS TO FINANCE YOUR EDUCATION

Financing your health care certificate program is not much different than financing a two- or four-year college degree. Under most circumstances, you can apply for federal grants, including a Pell Grant. Your first step would be to complete a FAFSA (Free Application for Federal Student Aid), which the federal government uses to identify the programs you are eligible for. You can also apply for public scholarships or private scholarships. For example, some schools offer their own scholarships (often named for a past student or faculty member) with their own specific criteria, and some health organizations offer scholarships in different health care fields that may coincide with your course of study.

There are many private grants you can also apply for. All you need is time to do an online search for grants in your field, and you never know what you might find. Of course, if all else fails, you can always finance your education with a student loan, your own personal savings, or the generosity of family and friends. When in doubt, check with your guidance or career counselor, or make a list of schools you're considering attending and contact each financial aid office to ask for help in identifying your options.

Medical doctors must show skill, precision, and compassion when working with patients. This doctor is examining a young man who was rushed to the emergency room.

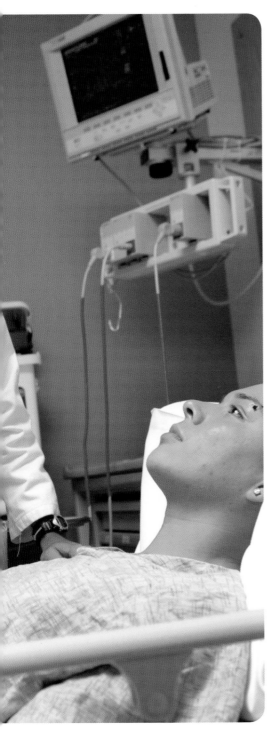

For example, if you were pursuing obstetrics and gynecology (OB/GYN), you would have already completed both your bachelor's and medical degrees. You would then be ready for an intensive three- to eight-year program that includes medical residency in a hospital or clinic, where you would gain hands-on knowledge and experience in your field.

It goes without saying that if you choose the five- to ten-year path, you are making a commitment to immersing yourself in your education. Any satisfactory employment would probably be delayed until you earn your degree. You would need personal finances or, at the very least, grants, scholarships, and fellowships in order to comfortably pursue your degree.

CHAPTER THREE

The Three Fastest-Growing Certificate Programs

The health care field is all about choices. In fact, the BLS reports that there are over thirteen million jobs and counting in the health care field. Luckily, this means you have plenty of jobs to choose from. You won't have to worry about whether you'll be needed; you'll only need to ponder how you will choose from among these jobs. You have to decide where to begin.

Perhaps the most logical way to begin is by examining the most popular health careers. Fortunately, the BLS has made this easier for you by identifying the three fastest-growing certified health care careers: home-health aides, medical assistants, and nursing aides and orderlies.

Home-Health Aides

According to the BLS, home-health aides held 875,000 jobs in the United States in 2012, proof that their skills were (and still are) definitely in demand. If you choose to become a home-health aide, you could work in a variety of settings, including private homes, adult day care facilities, retirement communities, and hospitals. Your clients would be the disabled, the chronically ill, the elderly, or the mentally challenged, and your hours would vary, depending upon the services needed. For example, you might work a regular shift (8 AM to 5 PM), or you might be needed overnight (11 PM to 7 AM). You might

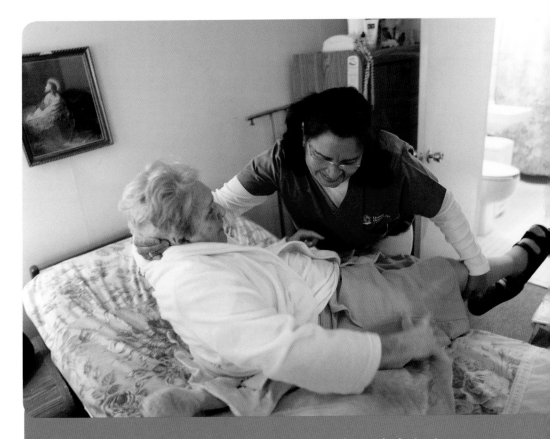

As a home-health aide, your patients may need your help to rise, remain standing, or walk. This aide needs strength and stamina to help this frail patient from the bed to the bathroom.

be needed only once a week, or you might be needed as a full-time live-in.

Home-health aides offer personal care like dressing, bathing, or grooming; cooking light meals; and helping clients keep their homes clean. You might transport clients from home to some designated activity center or doctor's office, and in some cases, you might be allowed to dispense medicine (like prescription pills) and document vital signs like blood pressure and body temperature.

According to O*Net Online, a database that offers prospective workers detailed information about the skills and prerequisites associated with various occupations, a home-health aide is usually charged with the task of "changing bandages, dressing wounds, and applying topical medications to the wounds of the elderly, the convalescent, or persons with disabilities, at the patient's home or in a care facility. They also monitor or report changes in health status."

Even though you don't necessarily need a high school diploma to perform the tasks described above, your employer might still insist that you at least have your GED and pass a standardized competency test. This is because you might also be expected to maintain client records, plan meals, read to or entertain clients, accompany a client to a doctor's appointment, or even direct a client in certain prescribed physical exercises. Because of these possible duties, a certain number of formalized training courses at a local vocational or community college would probably go well with on-the-job training (OJT) and mentoring.

Your typical day as a home-health aide might go something like this: you rise at 5 AM so that you can get to your elderly client's home by 6 AM to bathe, dress, and groom her so that she can be on the adult day care center bus promptly at 7 AM. While you wait with her for the bus to arrive, you ask her daughter, son, or guardian how she slept last night, what her toilet habits were like, whether she had any physical complaints, and whether she has eaten and taken her medications. You jot all this information down so that you can give it to the person who will work with her at the center where she is enrolled.

You may also have to follow the bus and help unload your client and get her safely inside the center. Once you leave the center, you check on other patients who are homebound or bedridden and help them with their toileting needs, too. You may then do a bit of grocery shopping for your clients, and when you return to their homes, you place the items in the refrigerator or cabinets where they belong. In some cases, you might prepare a meal or snack, help a client to the bathroom, or comb someone's hair before you leave.

By afternoon, you return to the center to check on the first client and see how she has fared during the day. You take down all important information, like whether she ate her food, socialized with others, or saw a doctor. Then you either telephone her family or follow the bus that takes her home so that you can tell her family firsthand about the type of day she has had. Once she is safely home with her guardians and you have dispersed any medicine, helped dress her, or recorded necessary information, you can finally go home.

These activities may not seem difficult, but home-health care can be physically exhausting. Your clients might be feeble, grossly overweight, or prone to wandering off. This means you would be constantly lifting or adjusting clients, or allowing them to lean on you for support while you maneuver them from one place to the other. You might also be constantly guiding the wandering client back to where he or she is supposed to be.

Medical Assistants

Although the title "medical assistant" may sound similar to "home-health aide," the two positions couldn't be more different. If you choose to become a medical assistant, you would be required to offer personal assistance, attend to medical needs, and give emotional support just like the home-health aide does. But that's as far as the similarities go.

As a medical assistant, you would be required to provide more advanced medical duties, like collecting blood, tissue, and other specimens. You might clean and sterilize instruments, perform routine lab tests, interview clients, write down their medical history and vital statistics, schedule appointments, maintain medical records, input information and data into a computer, and perform billing and coding for insurance companies.

Medical assistants are expected to know how to use tools like hypodermic needles, nebulizers, and manual blood pressure cuffs. You would need to be familiar with and understand compliance (whether events or processes comply with certain laws, standards, or regulations), and you would need to be

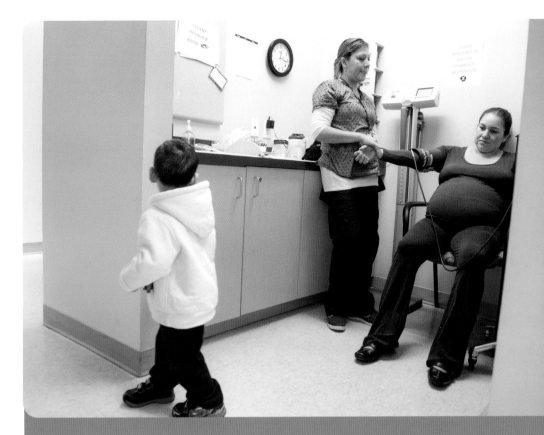

Record-keeping is an important part of most health care jobs. This medical assistant documents everything from blood pressure and weight to future appointments, and enters this data into the office computer.

comfortable communicating with coworkers, supervisors, and medical professionals.

To perform this vast number of duties, you would need to earn either a certificate or a two-year associate's degree from an accredited vocational school. Even when you do, you would still be expected to have prior or ongoing OJT under the supervision of other experienced medical professionals. You might even be encouraged to seek an internship to help prepare you to perform well. The internship, training courses, and OJT should arm you with—among other things—great speaking and listening skills, reading and writing comprehension, self-monitoring skills, critical thinking, and the confidence to speak and interact with others, no matter their technical or academic level.

The BLS claims that there were over 560,000 medical assistant jobs in 2012 and predicts that this field will grow 29 percent by the year 2022. This is great news where job security is concerned, but it should not be the only deciding factor for choosing to become a medical assistant. Keep in mind that the medical assistant's job is both challenging and exhausting, so if you choose this profession, you may be required to do more than just perform the above duties in a doctor's office; you may actually have to run the office.

A medical assistant's day would probably begin by entering the doctor's office or clinic an hour or more before the doctor arrives. You might check the office voicemail to determine whether there have been any emergencies, calls from patients or their families, or requests from other physicians or medical centers. If there are emergencies or requests, it might be your job to write the messages down for the physician or input client data into the physician's daily calendar. You might man the fax machine for incoming faxes, file any medical forms that need to be put away, fill out any pending forms, stock the supply cabinet, and answer the telephone whenever it rings.

You may have to weigh clients, take temperatures, check blood glucose (sugar) levels, guide clients to the

OTHER HEALTH CARE CERTIFICATES

The health care field is very broad, and you have a host of paths and certificates to choose from. For example, you can earn a certificate in end-of-life care, where you specialize in the emotional, physical, and medical care of the chronically or terminally ill. You can earn a gerontology certificate that gives you the skills to work with the nation's aging population (in this case, people over the age of sixty-five) and the issues they face, including mental health, Alzheimer's disease, and elder abuse. As a nurse or nursing assistant, you can even earn a certificate in oxygenation (also called issues in oxygenation), which, according to the Expert Rating website, trains you to recognize and treat "issues related to oxygenation assessment, intervention, and management." It takes six weeks to complete training in each of these specialties, which does not include the final examination to obtain the certificate.

exam room, and input data on vitals, medicines, and any other information into the computer. You might also schedule visits, set follow-up appointments, type letters, process insurance copayments, call the pharmacy, and make copies of necessary papers.

In other words, your day will likely be busy from the time you get to work until the time you leave. You may

Some health care professionals prefer running the office over interacting with patients. They answer the telephone, deliver messages, man the fax machine, fill out forms, and stock the supply cabinet.

even be on call after hours in case of an emergency. These are only a few of the factors you should consider as you ponder which health care job is right for you.

Nursing Assistants

A nursing assistant (nursing aide) position is quite different from the home-health aide and medical assistant positions. First of all, you would need to complete a state-approved education program at a community college, vocational school, or technical school, and you would need to pass your state's competency exam in order to be certified. With a satisfactory score on the competency exam, your name would be placed on a state registry, which would qualify you to work in a nursing home if you like.

After you pass the competency exam, you would

need to complete some sort of OJT specific to your place of employment. In other words, just any OJT wouldn't do; you would need to actually train at the place you plan to work (or a similar environment) so that you could learn the specifics of what your job would entail. You would also likely be subjected to a background check.

Once all these requirements are behind you, you could work at an assisted living facility or a retirement community. There, you would clean and bathe patients, help with daily living activities, help with toileting, measure and document vital statistics (blood pressure, blood glucose, etc.), prepare meals, and even help feed those who cannot feed themselves. If you worked at a nursing home, you might answer a call light or call button, change bed linens, physically turn patients onto their sides, help them sit up, and allow them to lean on you for balance as they walk. You might also ensure that patients' food trays include the exact diet their physicians have prescribed and that the patients are actually consuming the food. You might also comb patients' hair, measure and document their food and liquid intake, and document any complaints (physical, emotional, or medical) they may have.

The elderly population (people over the age of sixty-five) is steadily growing, and nursing assistant jobs are expanding right along with this population at an expected growth rate of 21 percent by the year 2022. In terms of job security, nursing assistants will be sorely needed to work with this population in long-term-care facilities. As long as the nursing assistant is compassionate and patient, has great communication skills, and is physically healthy and able to do quite a bit of lifting, he or she should thrive in this field.

Orderlies

Orderlies perform many of the same duties as nursing assistants. The only difference is that orderlies are not required to complete rigorous training courses or pass competency exams. They are typically subjected to a background check, but after that, a high school diploma or a GED is usually sufficient to land the job.

Orderlies perform a range of duties. They push wheelchairs and dress, feed, and even bathe some of their patients.

If you choose to become an orderly, you might transport patients via wheelchair to X-ray rooms or dining areas. You might stock supplies, answer call lights, deliver messages, change soiled bedding, clean equipment, or clean and sanitize a patient's room. You will typically be expected to know CPR, and you might even have to know how to use automated external defibrillators (hard paddles), which are used to shock a heart that has stopped.

You would be expected to provide excellent support to nursing assistants, nurses, home-health aides, physicians, or whomever you have the privilege of working with. You would also be expected to be patient and compassionate with your clients.

CHAPTER FOUR

Other Certificate Careers

f you didn't see anything you liked (in the way of professions) in the previous section, don't despair. There are still many interesting health care positions you can choose. For example, you might want to become a technician in one of the health care fields or pursue a career in office support.

Health Care Technicians

By definition, a technician is any individual who has earned a two-year degree (typically, but not under every circumstance) and who possesses specific skills in his or her own chosen field or profession. Following are descriptions of just a few of the many technician opportunities in health care.

Emergency Medical Technician/ Paramedic

If you feel that being a technician might be interesting, you might want to explore the world of the emergency medical technician (EMT) or paramedic. If you choose this field, your "office" would be the emergency medical vehicle and wherever your patient happens to be located. You would transport the sick and injured from their homes or the scene of an accident to the emergency room, and on the way, you would assess their injuries, administer first aid as needed, and operate machinery like defibrillators and electrocardiogram

EMTs transport critically ill or injured patients to medical facilities and often dispense medicines, use defibrillators, and practice other life-saving procedures along the way.

(EKG) machines. You would communicate a patient's vital signs to a dispatcher or treatment center to be sure that all is ready when the patient arrives at the hospital, and you would comfort the patient along the way. You might also have the not-so-pleasant job of decontaminating the ambulance after the patient exits the vehicle.

According to O*Net Online, there will be an estimated 121,000 jobs in this field between now and the year 2020, so there should be plenty of room for you to thrive. Keep in mind that you would need to complete a postsecondary degree in addition to state licensure, and you would probably be expected to attend various training or continuing education classes to ensure that your certificate is up to date and that you know all the latest procedures.

Occupational Health and Safety Technician

If you decide to become an occupational health and safety technician, you might work anywhere from "an office or factory to a coal mine," according to the BLS, where you would collect data, test the workplace for environmental hazards, plan emergency response drills, and help to direct firefighters in the event of a fire. You would need to monitor any situation in which any employee claims that the workplace is unsafe, and you would also conduct worker studies. You would inform the public about any public health hazards that might be present, and you might be called upon to work with schools or community programs to develop some sort of health standards. These are only a few of the broad range of skills and duties you would be expected to perform in this position. It is complex, detailed work, and it usually requires a bachelor's degree and specific OJT in inspection procedures. In addition, the job-growth outlook is much slower than others, but this position does pays extremely well and offers great job security.

Radiology Technician

If you decide to become a radiology technician, you would operate and maintain the equipment that is used to X-ray different areas of the body. Because you would work closely with patients—including transporting them to the X-ray rooms, explaining procedures, positioning them for the film, and reassuring them in the process—you would need excellent listening and communication skills, compassionate personal service, and attention to detail.

You might also maintain a log of daily activities. Your close work with physicians, nurses, and other technicians would require a high degree of professionalism and confidence in dealing with people on various levels of the academic ladder.

All of these "technician" fields require professionalism, integrity, precision, and attention to detail. They also require OJT in the field or environment in which you will be working and a two-year associate's degree (or, in the case of the radiology technician, a bachelor's degree).

INCREASED HIRING IN HEALTH CARE

Health care hiring is on the rise, and there are two main reasons why. First, the Affordable Care Act (ACA) is expected to result in an extra thirty-two million Americans having insurance coverage. Naturally, these thirty-two million people will need primary care physicians, nurse practitioners, nurses, and nursing assistants. They will also need non-contact personnel (people who work in health care but do not directly interact with patients) like billing and coding specialists, computer programmers, and record keepers. Second, people are living longer. There were more than forty million Americans over the age of sixty-five in 2010, and the baby boomers (those people born between 1946 and 1964) are turning sixty-five at the rate of ten thousand per day. This ever-expanding group of older people will need more medical care than their younger counterparts. In fact, according to an article by Tara Culp-Ressler, "The growing elderly population will require five million direct-care workers in 2020—nearly 50 percent more than the current workforce." This means that the need for nursing home, hospital, retirement home, assisted living, and medical care workers will only increase with time.

Dental

If you want to help people in pain but don't want to work the long, grueling hours of a physician, physician assistant, home-health aide, or CNA (certified nursing assistant), you might consider the field of dentistry. Except in extreme emergencies, dentists do not have to be on call and can work long or short hours, according to their whim. Their support staff would, of course, have the same work hours. But perhaps the best thing about going into dentistry is that dentists and their staffs are able to give back something that many of their patients thought they had lost forever: their confidence, their self-esteem, and their smiles.

Dental Assistant

To become a dental assistant, you would begin by earning your high school diploma, including early courses in biology, anatomy, or chemistry to "get your feet wet," so to speak. Then you would enroll in a course of one or more years in dental assisting from an accredited program (typically a vocational college) and obtain your certificate or diploma. You would also need to earn a certificate in CPR.

Some dental assistants are required to be licensed before they can work, so if you live in a state with this licensing requirement, you would earn this license by getting a passing score on the Certified Dental Assisting (CDA) exam. Afterward, you could begin working in a dentist's office, where you would receive OJT that includes learning to sterilize equipment, taking X-rays, making

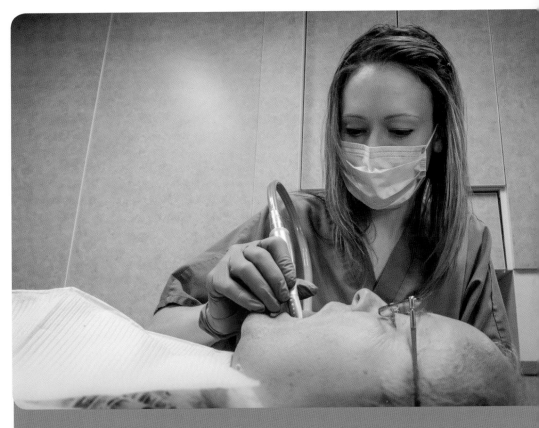

Dental assistants don face masks, gloves, and protective clothing to avoid contracting infections while working with patients. This assistant needs a good deal of stamina to bend over her patients for long periods of time.

casts of patients' teeth, keeping records of procedures, and instructing patients in proper dental care. Since there is always the possibility of contracting an infectious disease while performing dental procedures, you would probably wear a face mask, protective goggles, and protective clothing to ensure your safety as you perform the various procedures.

Dental Hygienist

To become a dental hygienist, you would need an associate's degree in dental hygiene and a license to practice your trade. You would begin the road to your career by taking biology, math, and chemistry classes in high school. Some states require at least one year of college before you enter the dental hygienist program, and others require enrollment in a vocational school where you take classes in radiology, chemistry, and periodontology (the study of gums), to name a few. If you were interested in an advanced degree in dental hygiene, earning a bachelor's or master's degree would qualify you to perform research or teach classes.

As for personal skills, you would need to be knowledgeable, compassionate, and detail-oriented. You would also need great stamina because you would probably be bending over patients for long periods of time. Your work environment would, of course, be a dentist's office, where you would wear protective gloves, goggles, a facial mask, and special clothing to avoid the possibility of catching an infectious disease. Although the U.S. Department of Labor states in its *Occupational Outlook Handbook* that the dental hygiene profession is expected to increase as much as 33 percent by the year 2022, most dental hygienists are only hired for part-time work, usually two to three days a week. For this reason, many dental hygienists work for more than one dentist at a time.

Lab Technician

According to the BLS, there are no formal educational requirements for becoming a dental lab technician. While you're completing your high school diploma, you might give special focus to science, math, art, and computer programming classes because these should give you a good head start in this chosen profession.

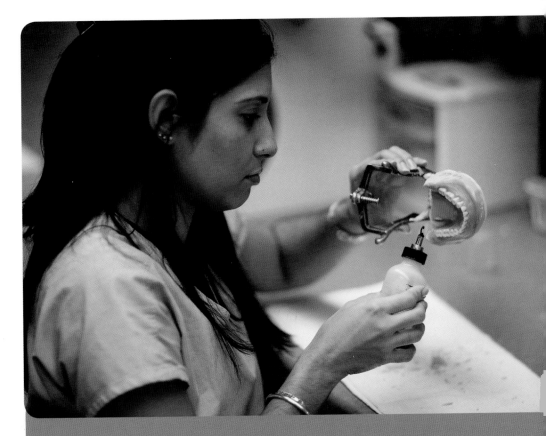

This dental lab technician is making a set of dentures that will give some lucky patient her smile back. Lab technicians also learn other important procedures, like making porcelain crowns.

After you graduate, you might enter a vocational or community college that offers a one-year program of instruction. Unfortunately, these one-year programs are very rare. It is more common for a dental lab technician to learn his or her job while completing OJT in the dental lab. During OJT, you might learn to pour plaster to make dental impressions (molds), and as your skills improve, you might move on to more advanced procedures, like making porcelain crowns.

Since every dental lab is different, every dental lab technician's OJT session will be different. However, to document your skill level or your years of OJT, you can earn a Certified Dental Technician (CDT) certificate from the National Board for Certification in Dental Laboratory Technology. This certificate is for technicians who specialize in skills that range from orthodontic appliances to dental implants. Technicians must have at least five years of OJT to qualify.

Office Support

Some health care positions do not involve interacting with patients. For example, if you choose to enter the field of office support, your job would be to provide clerical support that would help ensure that patients receive the highest-quality services, even if you're not the one actually serving them.

Medical Secretary

Hospitals, doctor's offices, health clinics, retirement homes, assisted living facilities, and the like all welcome someone who can make their busy office run like a well-oiled machine. If you choose to become a medical secretary, you would answer the telephone, schedule appointments, coordinate staff schedules, arrange meetings, draft and/or deliver messages, and offer other as-needed support to physicians, aides, technicians, and nurses.

Your work environment would be fast-paced and unpredictable. Your workday might begin as early as 6 AM (to accommodate working people) and end at 6 PM. On any given day, you might see dozens of sick, cranky, or impatient people, and you might have to deal with crying or frightened children or desperately ill older patients. For these reasons, you would need a patient and compassionate attitude. You would need to be understanding about the medical and emotional needs of sick people, and you would need to be a master at multitasking, since you might be answering the telephone, talking to patients, and listening to physicians and medical staff all at the same time.

To become a medical secretary, you would need to be a high school graduate. In some circumstances, you wouldn't necessarily need a certificate of any kind; rather, you could begin your job at the entry level and learn through OJT. This OJT would include learning the correct medical lingo (terminology), such as medical vocabulary and codes, to adequately understand the medical staff, and this training could take many months before you feel comfortable.

Under other circumstances, you might be required to enroll in a vocational or technical school where you would learn not only coding and terminology but also office procedures and medical software. This training might last for a year or more.

As a medical secretary, you would need great communication skills, good personal integrity, confidence to deal with professionals on all levels, and an easy-going personality so that busy offices and endless multitasking don't present a problem.

Medical Transcriptionist

If you like writing and dealing with various medical reports, you might consider becoming a medical transcriptionist. A medical transcriptionist typically works in a hospital or doctor's office where she may listen to dictation and transfer the information from voice recording to written report.

As busy doctors evaluate their patients during the day, they document their findings and opinions via voice recorders. These recorders are handed over to medical transcriptionists who are familiar with abbreviations, medical jargon, and medical codes. The transcriptionist listens to the doctor's verbal report and then writes a detailed diagnostic report, referral letter, or other document.

Since you would be writing, reviewing, and editing written or verbal drafts, you must have excellent writing, listening, computer, and critical thinking skills. You must also have excellent time-management skills, especially if you work at home, as many medical transcriptionists do.

If this seems like your dream job, you must first complete high school, then enroll in a vocational school,

Medical coders must be very organized and detail-oriented in order to perform their jobs well. The codes this medical coder is entering into a patient's records will eventually be accessed by insurance companies.

community college, or distance-learning program for postsecondary training. There, you should learn anatomy, physiology, computer skills, and medical terminology. You should also do well in English grammar and become familiar with the legal issues surrounding health care documentation. Your program of choice may last from one to two years, and during or immediately after that time, you should receive well-supervised OJT.

Although laws may vary from state to state, medical transcriptionists are not typically required to be certified. However, certificates are available for those who are ambitious enough to pursue them. In that case, you could earn a Registered Health Care Documentation Specialist (RHDS) certificate, which is for recent graduates who have less than two years of experience, or a Certified Health Care Documentation Specialist (CHDS) certificate, which is for graduates with two or more years of experience and who handle two or more medical specialties. Both these certificates require retesting to stay abreast of changes.

There were approximately 84,100 medical transcriptionist jobs in 2012, and the profession is expected to grow as much as 8 percent by the year 2022.

Medical Records and Health Information Technician

If you are very organized and like reading and reviewing data, you might consider entering the medical records and health information technician field.

A health information technician documents a patient's entire medical record. For example, the technician records patient complaints, symptoms, treatments, and test results. Although this job does not entail working directly with patients, the health information technician does work closely with RNs, physicians, and other personnel in order to make patient records as complete as possible.

Some health information technicians specialize as medical coders and cancer registrars. Both specialties include reviewing records for accuracy and completeness, but one (medical coder) is a liaison with medical billing offices, and the other (cancer registrar) compiles information for cancer research.

To become a health information technician, you would begin by taking computer science, math, health, and biology classes in high school. After you graduate, you would need an associate's degree or a postsecondary degree that includes courses in anatomy and physiology, classification and coding systems, medical terminology, health data requirements and standards, and health care statistics, to name a few. In addition, you would need to understand and be able to use electronic health records (EHR) software, which is integrated into most medical offices and is strongly advocated by the federal government. Your employer might also require you to possess a professional certificate like the Registered Health Information Technician (RHIT) or Certified Tumor Registrar (CTR). These certificates may be earned from an accredited program and would be renewed via continuing education courses.

As for job outlook, the health information technician field is expected to increase at least 22 percent by the year 2022. This is because the aging population is sure to need more tests and procedures that will translate into more medical claims. According to the BLS, those health information technicians who go on to earn the professional certificates mentioned above have the best chance for snagging these jobs.

CHAPTER FIVE

Degree Careers

Your examination of the health care field would not be complete without exploring a few degreed careers. If you have a deep desire to nurture, heal, or have some type of direct involvement in the health and well-being of other humans, you might want to consider an advanced degree in health care. Even if you don't plan to go that far in your education, it's still good to know what's out there, just in case.

Physicians and Surgeons

To become a physician or surgeon, you would need an intensive, extensive education. Intensive means your courses would be detailed, your internships would be nonstop and fast-paced, and the competition to train in the best schools or hospitals would be fierce. Extensive means your formal education would last for many, many years. You would need a bachelor's degree (four years) to apply for medical school (four more years), and after medical school you would enter your internship or residency (three to eight more years).

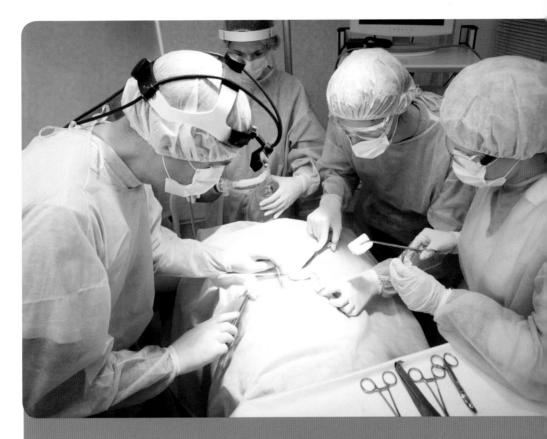

Physicians and surgeons must commit to a decade or more of education and hands-on practice to perform the complex, fast-paced, and demanding duties that are a part of their everyday regimen.

If these numbers don't discourage you, and you still want to become a physician or surgeon (even if only in the far-off future), you should know the difference between the two professions. According to the BLS, physicians "examine patients; take medical histories; prescribe medications; order, perform, and interpret diagnostic tests; and counsel patients on diet, hygiene, and preventive health care." Surgeons operate on patients.

If you became a surgeon or physician, you could set up and work in your own private office, or you could work in a hospital or clinic. The work environment would be fast-paced and would include long daily hours, late night or early morning calls, and weekends "on call." These conditions are the reasons many physicians merge with other physicians to start a physician's group so that their patient load is spread among many doctors.

Employment for physicians and surgeons is expected to grow at least 18 percent by the year 2022. This is largely due to the aging baby-boomer generation and the fact that Americans are living longer, which often results in more medical needs.

Nurses (RNs, LPNs, and LVNs)

To become a registered nurse (RN), you would need to enroll in a broad assortment of courses, including chemistry, nutrition, microbiology, and, of course, anatomy. You would even need to take certain psychology and behavioral science courses. With these and other required courses, you could earn an associate's degree (ADN), a bachelor's degree (BSN), or a diploma from some other preapproved nursing program. Even with these professional courses behind you, you may still be subject to additional licensing requirements, depending upon the state you live in.

As an RN, you might work in a hospital, a doctor's office, a nursing home, a day center for the elderly, or a government office. These settings are fast-paced and often hectic, and you would need an excellent set of professional and personal skills to endure. For example, you would need compassion, patience, a strong constitution, good speaking skills, and excellent attention to detail. You would also need to be emotionally stable, have good physical stamina, and have great leadership skills in order to thrive.

There is room to branch out in nursing. For example, some RNs go on to become midwives (who are trained to assist in childbirth) or nurse practitioners (who can treat certain conditions without a doctor's supervision).

The registered nurse profession is expected to grow by about 19 percent by the year 2022. Again, this growth will be due to aging baby boomers who will need more medical care. It will also be influenced by the fact that Americans are living much longer and will need more medicine, medical tests, and procedures as they live on.

An LPN is a licensed practical nurse, and an LVN is a licensed vocational nurse. Both of these categories of nurses are involved in basic patient care. They monitor patients, keep medical records, change bandages, and check blood pressure and other vital statistics, all under the direct supervision of RNs. They may even help deliver or feed newborn babies.

LPNs and LVNs usually complete some type of one-year state-approved program, so if you are interested in nursing but don't want to enroll in a long-term program, you might consider these professions. Job growth is expected to be at least 25 percent by the year 2022, but there may be even more jobs for LPNs and LVNs if they are willing to practice in rural or isolated areas.

Dieticians and Nutritionists

If you like to cook and believe you can help people eat healthy and balanced meals, you might want to become a dietician or nutritionist. After you obtain a bachelor's degree and undergo a supervised internship (and after you become licensed, if your state requires it), you would be ready to work full- or part-time in a hospital, nursing home, school, cafeteria, or residential facility.

If you want more flexibility, you might choose to work as a self-employed dietitian. In this capacity, you would choose your own hours to consult with patients, contract yourself out to health care facilities, or help individuals develop a healthy meal plan.

The job outlook for this profession is very positive, largely because of the high numbers of obese Americans. Obesity is known to cause many devastating illnesses, including diabetes and kidney disease. To diminish or completely avoid the negative results associated with obesity, dietitians and nutritionists are needed to customize appropriate meal plans and help patients learn healthy eating habits.

Physician Assistant

If you aren't quite committed enough to become a doctor but still dream of practicing medicine, you might consider becoming a physician assistant.

To become a physician assistant, you would need a master's degree from an accredited school. This

This registered dietician works as a nutritionist at a residential facility, where she plans healthy and balanced meals for patients who are obese or diabetic or who have poor eating habits.

means you would need at least six years of college (four years in undergraduate work and an additional two years for your master's program). You would also need to have taken health care–related coursework. For example, most physician assistants have RN or EMT backgrounds and have hundreds of hours of clinical training. No matter what degree you have, you would have to be licensed by passing the Physician

CAREERS IN ALTERNATIVE MEDICINE (NATUROPATHY AND ACUPUNCTURE)

If you are one of those people who likes doing things differently, you might pursue a career in alternative medicine. Alternative medicine is any medical therapy that is not considered "routine" or that has not been proven via the standard scientific methods. These therapies include naturopathy and acupuncture.

If you become a naturopathic doctor (ND), you would attend a four-year naturopathic school where you would study the underlying causes of disease and focus heavily on disease prevention. This might include the use of diet, lifestyle, and herbal recipes and remedies to promote good health.

If you are interested in acupuncture, you would first need to have two to four years of college under your belt, then an additional four years of study at an accredited institute of acupuncture and Oriental medicine. Of course, requirements differ from state to state, but whatever the length, you would complete your study with the knowledge of how to treat pain by inserting needles into certain areas of the skin or tissue.

Assistant National Certifying Examination (PANCE). You would also need to complete one hundred hours of continuing education courses every ten years.

To become a physician assistant, this woman earned a master's degree and passed the Physician Assistant National Certifying Examination (PANCE). She can now work in a variety of medical settings, including this low-cost clinic.

Once you complete all this rigorous training, you could work in medical offices, hospitals, outpatient centers, and various branches of the government. Your work environment would be quite hectic and would include working in operating rooms, making rounds, and standing on your feet all day.

Employment is expected to increase by at least 38 percent (by 2022) because of the nation's aging population and the medical needs of the aging baby-boomer generation.

CHAPTER SIX

Lifelong Learning Possibilities

esearchers say that knowledge doubles in every field (including health care) every two to three years. This is easy enough to understand. We live in the information age, where seekers and learners can digitally travel anywhere on the globe in nanoseconds and knowledge can be accessed at the click of a button. With all this knowledge at our fingertips, it's easy to be a lifelong learner. But what exactly is a lifelong learner?

Lifelong learning is the concept that learning and education are not confined to a classroom or to a person's place of employment but are a part of that person's entire life—from the cradle to the grave. A lifelong learner is a lifelong student—someone who devotes himself or herself to learning whatever adds to his or her skills and expertise, whenever the opportunity presents itself.

When you become a lifelong learner, you set about learning for the sake of learning. You understand that no matter how old you are, no matter how good you become at your job, there is always something new to

Consider becoming a lifelong learner who keeps up with the latest information, procedures, and trends in your profession. This way, your mind will stay sharp and you will remain well-versed in your field.

learn. Therefore, you commit yourself to learning. You commit yourself to keeping up with new information, procedures, and trends through continuing education courses, seminars, or postsecondary schooling. But even as you do, you never forget that the things you learn should also be used to better your personal life, your environment, your family, your workplace, and the people you encounter every day.

This means that some things you learn may be directly related to your profession and lead to stronger employment stability and better earning power. Other things you learn may not involve health care but may serve to broaden your horizons, feed your creative side, and enhance your personal well-being. All these things make you a happier, well-rounded person who is more skilled, more informed, and a better member of society. Learning new things (whatever they are) keeps your brain sharp and may even place you at or near the front of the promotion line. You may even become eligible for a raise.

Some employers are happy to take an active role in your lifelong learning by financing or reimbursing your courses. They do this because they know that a better, more skillful, newly improved you will spill over into the workplace and make it a more efficient environment with happier clients and coworkers. Other employers may not offer guidance but leave you to your own devices in choosing your continuing education courses. They may or may not reimburse you for the continuing education courses you take. Whatever the case, be aware that bettering yourself is your own responsibility, and your success will depend upon your personal commitment and your ability to monitor your own progress.

Steps to Becoming a Lifelong Learner

There are many ways to become a lifelong learner, but these steps may help you focus:

1. Read as many books or articles as you can find that are related to your job.
2. Find books that aren't related to your job and read them for enjoyment.
3. Join online and offline groups to network with others in your profession.
4. Join classes or groups that interest you but are not related to your job.
5. Keep a running list of things you've

These home care associates are attending a free course in their community. Find your perfect lifelong learning course by checking with your employer or conducting an Internet search via your favorite search engine.

always wanted to learn and places you've always wanted to go, and check them off as you accomplish them.

6. Ask questions about everything that interests you.

7. Ask your employer (or teacher) to allow you to learn something new, like a software program, even if it has nothing to do with your job.

8. Attend lectures, seminars, and free online webinars whenever you get the opportunity.

9. Find a mentor and ask for hands-on advice and experience.

10. Decide where you want to be in terms of learning and then map out the steps it will take to get there.

Continuing Education Programs

There are a host of lifelong learning programs all across the United States. Many of these programs are housed at area community colleges or vocational colleges. If you want to get a sense of just how many of these programs exist nationwide, enter keywords like "lifelong learning through continuing education" or "online lifelong learning" in Google or other popular search engines. These keywords will produce thousands of useful results that you can browse for a feel of the type of courses being offered. You can further tweak the results by adding the name of your own city and state to the keywords, and this should give you a good idea of the programs that are available at a location near you.

Make a list of the schools that interest you and the courses they offer. You can discuss your findings with your guidance or career counselor or, if you're already working, your employer. Click the links to learn more, or contact the school by e-mail or telephone to discuss your learning plans.

Again, you may have the type of employer who believes in investing in lifelong learning courses for his or her workers. In that case, your class fees would either be financed on the front end or reimbursed after successful completion. Alternately, you may qualify for some type of financial aid, but if not, you may have to pay for your courses out of your own pocket or via loans from friends or family.

If you do pay for courses out of your own pocket, you may qualify for certain tax cuts when tax time rolls around. The lifetime learning tax credit is available for college students, professional degree students, and students enrolled in at least one course that will lead to improved job skills or a certificate.

The health care field is wide open and full of possibilities. If you want to make a career of it—or even if you only think you do—your first move should be to explore the many positions in the field to see which may be right for you. Once you make your choice, just do your best and dream of ways to make it (and your own life) better through lifelong learning.

GLOSSARY

administrative Related to managing a business or organization.

baby boomer Any person born after World War II, between the years 1946 and 1964.

clerical Of or related to any job duties that are performed in an office or that involve desk work.

clinical Of or related to any medical work (usually performed in a hospital or clinic) that involves directly observing a patient as a component of diagnosis and treatment.

constitution A person's physical condition and his or her ability to stay well.

core classes Those subjects or courses that are required study in a particular educational program.

CPR Cardiopulmonary resuscitation; a series of chest compressions that prolongs the life of a nonbreathing, unresponsive person by helping to move oxygen-carrying blood to the person's brain and vital organs.

cradle to the grave From birth to death; a person's entire lifetime.

defibrillator A machine that applies an electric current to the heart (or heart wall) and shocks the heart.

dispatcher A person in charge of receiving and transmitting (sending out) important messages.

EKG Electrocardiogram; a test that checks to see if there are any problems with a heart's electrical activity.

elective A class that is not required but is an option chosen by the student.

FAFSA The Free Application for Federal Student Aid (FAFSA); a form used to determine what grants, scholarships, fellowships, or internships a student may be eligible for.

integrity Being honest and having strong morals.

internship A temporary position that usually offers a type of entry-level, on-the-job training for career professionals and that often offers financial compensation.

lingo The special words or vocabulary in a particular field of study.

obese Describing a person whose body fat and weight are considered adverse and possibly deadly.

OJT On-the-job training.

orthodox Of or related to a way of doing things that is considered accepted and true by most people.

postsecondary degree Any degree that you obtain after high school.

prerequisite Describing any classes that are required to be taken and passed before other classes can be taken.

stamina Ability to sustain prolonged physical or mental effort.

streamlined Designed to be more efficient or simple by removing unnecessary elements.

terminology The technical terms used in a field.

work ethic Dedication to hard work and diligence.

FOR MORE INFORMATION

American Medical Association (AMA)
AMA Plaza
330 N. Wabash Avenue
Chicago, IL 60611-5885
(800) 621-8335
Website: http://www.ama-assn.org
This organization is dedicated to advancing medical
science and public health through publications and
various programs.

American Public Health Association (APHA)
800 I Street NW
Washington, DC 20001
(202) 777-2742
Website: http://www.apha.org
This organization provides resources for professionals
in the public health field and advocates for public
health issues.

Association of American Medical Colleges (AAMC)
Aspiring Docs Program
2450 N Street NW
Washington, DC 20037
(202) 828-0400
Website: https://www.aamc.org/students/aspiring
This program provides inspiration and resources to
anyone aspiring to be a physician.

Association of Faculties of Medicine
of Canada (AFMC)

265 Carling Avenue, Suite 800
Ottawa, ON K1S 2E1
Canada
(613) 730-0687
Website: http://www.afmc.ca
This organization supports Canadian faculties of medicine, staff, and learners. It promotes excellence in health care and medical education and research across Canada.

Canadian Public Health Association (CPHA)
404-1525 Carling Avenue
Ottawa, ON K1Z 8R9
Canada
(613) 725-3769
Website: http://www.cpha.ca
The CPHA represents the public health issues of Canada and advises decision makers in key policy areas.

HOSA: Future Health Professionals
548 Silicon Drive, Suite 101
Southlake, TX 76092
(800) 321-4672
Website: http://www.hosa.org
The HOSA aims to provide students in the field of health science with educational resources, leadership training, and motivation as they pursue career opportunities in health care.

National Student Leadership Conference (NSLC)
Medicine & Health Care
320 W. Ohio Street, Suite 4W

Chicago, IL 60654
(800) 994-6752
Website: http://www.nslcleaders.org
The NSLC allows students interested in health care to gain firsthand experience in the field by visiting medical facilities, meeting professionals, participating in simulations, and more. Students also gain valuable leadership skills.

National Youth Leadership Forum: Careers in Medicine
Envision Office of Admissions
1101 Pennsylvania Avenue NW, Suite 600
Washington, DC 20004
(877) 587-9659
Website: http://www.envisionexperience.com /explore-our-programs/careers-in-medicine #what-to-expect
This program is designed for the highest-achieving high school students to gain real-world medical career experience and to explore professional career opportunities in medicine and health care.

Websites

Because of the changing nature of Internet links, Rosen Publishing has developed an online list of websites related to the subject of this book. This site is updated regularly. Please use this link to access the list:

http://www.rosenlinks.com/RDFM/Heal

FOR FURTHER READING

American Medical Association. *Health Care Careers Directory 2012–2013*. Chicago, IL: American Medical Association, 2012.

Askin, Elizabeth, and Nathan Moore. *The Health Care Handbook*. St. Louis, MO: Washington University in St. Louis, 2012.

Brooks, Myrna LaFleur, and Danielle LaFleur Brooks. *Exploring Medical Language: A Student-Directed Approach*. St. Louis, MO: Elsevier, 2011.

Christen, Carol, and Richard N. Bolles. *Discovering Yourself, Defining Your Future* (What Color Is Your Parachute? For Teens). New York, NY: Ten Speed Press, 2010.

Farr, Michael, and Laurence Shatkin. *300 Best Jobs Without a Four-Year Degree*. Indianapolis, IN: JIST Works, 2013.

Friedman, Leonard H., and Anthony R. Kovner. *101 Careers in Healthcare Management*. New York, NY: Springer Publishing, 2013.

Gerdin, Judith. *Health Careers Today*. St. Louis, MO: Elsevier, 2011.

Lore, Nicholas. *Now What?: The Young Person's Guide to Choosing the Perfect Career*. New York, NY: Fireside, 2008.

McClure, Christopher, and Jessica McClure. *Your Job Search Is Over: Résumé Building and Interview Prep in a Healthcare World*. Jacksonville, FL: MedEd Premier, 2013.

Mitchell, Dakota, and Lee Haroun. *Introduction to Health Care*. Clifton Park, NY: Delmar, 2012.

O'Sullivan, Vanessa. *Basic Training for Careers in Health Care*. Seattle, WA: Amazon Digital Services, Inc., 2010.

Peterson's. *Teens' Guide to College & Career Planning*. Lawrenceville, NJ: Peterson's, 2011.

Pierce, Valerie, and Cheryl Rilly. *Countdown to College: 21 "To Do" Lists for High School*. Haslett, MI: Front Porch Press, 2009.

Quan, Kathy. *The Everything Guide to Careers in Health Care: Find the Job That's Right for You*. Avon, MA: Adams Media, 2006.

Seltzer, Beth. *Careers in Public Health*. New York, NY: Springer Publishing, 2011.

Shatkin, Laurence. *Best Jobs for the 21st Century*. Indianapolis, IN: JIST Works, 2011.

Tieger, Paul, and Barbara Barron-Tieger. *Do What You Are: Discover the Perfect Career for You Through the Secrets of Personality Type*. New York, NY: Little, Brown and Company, 2007.

U.S. Department of Labor. *Occupational Outlook Handbook 2013–2014*. New York, NY: Skyhorse Publishing, 2012.

Wischnitzer, Saul, and Edith Wischnitzer. *Top 100 Health-care Careers*. Indianapolis, IN: JIST Works, 2010.

Zichy, Shoya. *Career Match: Connecting Who You Are with What You'll Love to Do*. New York, NY: AMACOM, 2007.

BIBLIOGRAPHY

American College of Health Care Executives. "Health Care: A Changing System." Retrieved January 20, 2014 (https://www.ache.org/carsvcs/ycareer.cfm).

Cheney, Alexandra. "A Career in Health Care." *Wall Street Journal*, September 13, 2010. Retrieved January 20, 2014 (http://online.wsj.com/news/articles/SB10001424052748703946504575469840721907252).

Culp-Ressler, Tara. "As Boomers Age, Nursing Homes Face a Growing Shortage." ThinkProgress.org, April 16, 2013. Retrieved January 20, 2014 (http://thinkprogress.org/health/2013/04/16/1866911/baby-boomers-home-health-shortage).

Ellis, Janice Rider, and Celia Love Hartley. *Nursing in Today's World*. Philadelphia, PA: Wolters Kluwer Health, 2011.

Expert Rating. "Online Oxygenation Skills Certifaction." Retrieved January 20, 2014 (http://www.expertrating.com/certifications/InstructorLed/Health-Care-Continuing-Education/Oxygenation-Issues-Certificate-in/Oxygenation-Issues-Certificate-in.asp).

ExploreHealthCareers.org. "Top 10 Reasons to Pursue a Health Career Now." Retrieved January 20, 2014 (http://explorehealthcareers.org/en/issues/news/Article/178/Top_10_Reasons_to_Pursue_a_Health_Career_Now).

Friedman, Leonard H., and Anthony R. Kovner. *101 Careers in Healthcare Management*. New York, NY: Springer Publishing Company, 2013.

Gerdin, Judith. *Health Careers Today*. St. Louis, MO: Elsevier, 2011.

Gerdin, Judith. *Workbook for Health Careers Today*. St. Louis, MO: Elsevier, 2011.

Josiah Macy Jr. Foundation. Retrieved January 20, 2014 (www.josiahmacyfoundation.org).

O*Net Online. Retrieved January 20, 2014 (http://www.onetonline.org).

Open Education Database. "The Self-Directed Student Toolbox: 100 Web Resources for Lifelong Learners." Retrieved January 20, 2014 (http://oedb.org/ilibrarian/the-self-directed-student-toolbox-100-web-resources-for-lifelong-learners).

Seltzer, Beth. *Careers in Public Health*. New York, NY: Springer Publishing, 2011.

Strayer, Pam. "10 Reasons to Get into a Health Care Career." AllHealthCare. Retrieved January 20, 2014 (http://allhealthcare.monster.com/careers/articles/127-10-reasons-to-get-into-a-healthcare-career).

U.S. Bureau of Labor Statistics. "Home Health Aides." *Occupational Outlook Handbook*. Retrieved January 20, 2014 (http://www.bls.gov/ooh/healthcare/home-health-aides.htm).

U.S. Bureau of Labor Statistics. *Occupational Outlook Handbook*. Retrieved January 20, 2014 (http://www.bls.gov/ooh/healthcare/home.htm).

U.S. Department of Labor. "Fastest Growing Occupations." December 13, 2013. Retrieved January 20, 2014 (http://www.bls.gov/emp/ep_table_103.htm).

Wischnitzer, Saul, and Edith Wischnitzer. *Top 100 Health-care Careers*. Indianapolis, IN: JIST Works, 2010.

INDEX

About the Author

Rita Lorraine Hubbard was a special educator for over twenty years who taught academically challenged and exceptional children social and survival skills to help them transition to the work world. She is the author of several nonfiction books and one historical fiction picture book. She also reviews books for major trade publishers across the United States, provides book reviews for the *New York Journal of Books*, and occasionally works as an editor.

Photo Credits

Cover (figure) Minerva Studio/Shutterstock.com; cover (background) Poznyakov/Shutterstock.com; back cover, pp. 7, 15, 24, 37, 52, 61 YanLev/Shutterstock.com; p. 1 Lisa S./Shutterstock.com; pp. 4–5 (background) hxdbzxy/Shuttestock.com; p. 5 Bloomberg/Getty Images; p. 8 Mike Watson Images/moodboard/Thinkstock; p. 10 Newport News Daily Press/McClatchey-Tribune/Getty Images; p. 12 michaeljung/iStock/Thinkstock; p. 14 Yobro10/iStock/Thinkstock; p. 16 Digital Vision/Photodisc/Getty Images; pp. 19, 29 The Washington Post/Getty Images; pp. 20, 25, 45 Joe Raedle/Getty Images; pp. 22–23 Kart Gehring/Denver Post/Getty Images; pp. 32–33 Stockbyte/Thinkstock; p. 35 Catherine Yeulet/iStock/Thinkstock; p. 38 Kathryn Scott Osler/Denver Post/Getty Images; p. 43 Denise Bird/iStock/Thinkstock; p. 49 Miami Herald/McClatchey-Tribune/Getty Images; p. 53 mediaphotos/iStock/Thinkstock; p. 57 Helen H. Richardson/Denver Post/Getty Images; p. 59 John Moore/Getty Images; p. 62 © AP Images; pp. 64–65 New York Daily News Archive/Getty Images; additional cover and interior design elements PremiumVector/Shutterstock.com, Mike McDonald/Shutterstock.com (emblem components), Milena_Bo/Shutterstock.com, ririro/Shutterstock.com, The_Pixel/Shutterstock.com, Zffoto/Shutterstock.com, Rafal Olechowski/Shutterstock.com (banners, backgrounds).

Designer: Michael Moy; Editor: Shalini Saxena; Photo Researcher: Amy Feinberg